A Beginner's Guide to

CRYSTAL HEALING & THE FIVE ELEMENTS OF TRADITIONAL CHINESE MEDICINE

MARION McGEOUGH

Published by Marion McGeough.

A CIP Catalogue record for this book is available from the British Library.

Formatting and cover design by ebook-designs.co.uk

INTRODUCTION:

Welcome

Imagine that you have now entered a new world. In this world you will find that doctors would only get paid if they kept people well. If a person became sick the doctor had failed. Just imagine how wonderful life would be to live in a society like that. Now, this is not a claim by a politician in order to be elected nor is it an advertisement for a healthcare provider, this is what life was like in ancient China.

Ever since I can remember, I have been interested in health and wellbeing. When I was a child I had the unusual ability to just know when someone was sick or even, on the rare occasion, when someone was going to die. As I grew and developed I began to ignore that special part of myself. It was like someone kept knocking at the door and I refused to listen until one day they gave up. I had many jobs and eventually I became interested in Reiki after the death of my mother. I was very drawn to work with the energy and found that I was able to not only feel where the energy blockages were but I was also able to detect emotions, feel blockages within the meridians and receive messages from loved ones who had crossed over.

Each of us is truly an individual. We are unique as a species. Each of us is made up of different life experiences. Along with genetic variables and personal preferences we try to fit into society forgetting this uniqueness. Modern medicine is simply that, modern. The five Elements were first noted almost two thousand five hundred years ago. The Five Elements are found in nature as are crystals, beautiful and natural structures made by Mother Nature herself. Crystals, when used correctly can be used to help correct the imbalances within the body.

This book is divided into three sections:

The first explains in simple terms what the Five Elements are and you will be introduced to the archetypes of each of the Five Elements. The archetypes are simply personality types. As you progress with your reading, you will be able to identify your archetype. Once you have discovered what this is you will be able to detect where in your body any imbalance is present.

The second section will introduce you to the basics of crystal healing: You will learn how to purchase, use and clean crystals.

The third section will show you how you can help to heal yourself. I have selected ten of the most powerful crystals to assist the healing process for each of the Five Elements. You are also guided on how to carry out a crystal healing treatment for each of the five archetypes.

This book is only a short guide. It is not my aim to swamp you with lots of information that you most likely will not use, even be interested in or even worse feel overwhelmed and simply put the book on the bookshelf , not bothering to read it again. What a waste! This book is intended to act as a practical guide offering you guidance on how to help improve your health.

I wish you joy, good health and happiness on your journey of self- discovery.

THE FIVE ELEMENTS: THE BASICS

The Five Elements are based on the core aspects of Chinese Medicine. The core aspects of Chinese medicine are Yin and Yang, Qi and Jing and Shen. Each of these aspects are explained below.

Yin and Yang: These are two opposite but complementary forces. Yin is dark and is often expressed as night and is a female energy, Yang is day and is male energy. Although they are opposite they are never completely so. It is all about balance – nothing is completely Yin or completely Yang. Within the human body it is possible to have an excess of either Yin or Yang. Chinese medicine can work to correct these imbalances along with crystals which can be used for specific ailments to help the body achieve the correct vibrational frequency. A person with a fever for example, has too much Yang energy. Amber is a great crystal to help clear any imbalances connected to a fever as well as helping to reduce aches and pains in the joints, common symptoms of those with a fever.

Qi: This is pronounced "chee" and may be written as either chi or ki, as there are Japanese and Chinese variants. Qi is your life force, it is universal life energy. Qi is essential to the life of all living things, with human beings its function is to move around the body energising it. When this energy becomes blocked illness develops. Qi is also the energy which is used during a Reiki treatment. The Reiki practitioner has been connected to the universal life energy by a specific ritual or set of rituals carried out by the Reiki Master/teacher. The practitioner is then able to act as a vessel, simply by being neutral and allowing the energy to flow through themselves and to the recipient to assist in healing.

Jing: At the prenatal stage Jing is passed from mother to fetus via the kidneys. This process continues throughout development until birth. Jing contains the mothers DNA which is fixed and cannot be changed. Jing is stored in the kidneys.

Shen: This is the spiritual aspect of our selves that is connected to our consciousness, emotions and our thoughts. A well balanced person will have a deep connection with the world and view the world objectively. A sense of balance in all things will enable us to do this. Healthy living, good food, a sense of purpose and exercise will help to maintain this balance. Anxiety, depression and insomnia are the result of an imbalance. Rose quartz is a great crystal to help to heal the heart. The heart is deeply connected with the spirit.

Each person is also born with a specific purpose in life. The path to this purpose can vary greatly. If a person is, say for example, destined towards the caring professions they may choose a career in human or animal medicine or they may work as a care assistant, a care manager or in the field of mental health. The further away from our path we stray the greater the imbalance becomes. We often know deep down inside of ourselves when something feels right and when something feels wrong. There are many other ways that an imbalance can be created from within. A person may suffer abuse or a childhood trauma, they may be an abusive relationship, they may feel restricted creatively or by the job that they do. When an imbalance is felt within, the result is an imbalance within the Five Elements. Energy becomes blocked, the person feels discomfort and that something is not quite right. Illness and dis-ease follow. I hope that you are now beginning to understand that it is not the illness that comes first and the person then appears to be symptomatic of that illness but the imbalance from within, the disharmony arises first and the dis-ease then follows.

The five elements themselves are as follows: wood, fire, earth, metal and water. Everything of and within the earth is made of varying combinations of these five elements. In a person, each element corresponds to an organ. Wood corresponds to the liver and the gallbladder.

Fire corresponds to the heart and the small intestine. Earth corresponds to the stomach and the spleen. Metal corresponds to the lungs and the colon. Water corresponds to the bladder and the kidneys. Each of the five elements also corresponds to a specific season, planet, emotion and colour. There are other associations that are made by acupuncturists and doctors of Chinese medicine but I have chosen to list the basic ones to help you get to grips with the Five Elements. Running through all of the organs is Qi, life energy. Just as energy is constantly flowing and changing, the energy flowing through our bodies can also change. You may have too much or too little Qi flowing through a particular organ. With an understanding of the five elements and the use of the correct crystals to help support the organ that has become imbalanced, it is possible to restore good health once more.

As well as the five elements themselves there are also the five archetypes. These are simply the five different and most common patterns of personality and behaviours that have been identified throughout the world. If there is an imbalance in your archetype you will be affected on all levels: physically, mentally and emotionally. As you progress through this book you will be able to identify your archetype and identify any imbalance that you have in that particular area of the body and take the necessary steps to help restore good health. Remember that all of the organs of the body are linked by the flow of blood and Qi, so if there is an imbalance in one area you may eventually have an imbalance in another area. Alternatively, you may find that after you have identified your archetype that you are in perfect health. If this is you, simply knowing that you are on the right track will act as positive re-enforcement for you to keep up the good work!

A Body Scan Meditation

I have included a body scan meditation for you to carry out before you read about the Five Elements in greater detail. The body scan meditation will allow you to develop a greater connection to what is actually going on inside your body. All too often we tend to focus on what is happening on the outside and not what is going on within.

If you are new to meditation please read the following section, if you are not, skip directly to the meditation itself.

Find a quiet place where you will not be disturbed.

Remember to turn off your electronic devices so that you will not be distracted and leave them in another room. This is your time after all and you deserve some peace and relaxation in your life!

You may wish to use scented candles, play subtle, relaxing music and close the curtains/turn down the lights. All of this will add to a relaxing, calming atmosphere.

Find somewhere comfortable to sit down. You may wish to sit on your favourite chair or even the floor. Wherever you choose to sit ensure that you are sitting up straight. This does not mean that you have sit up ramrod straight as this is an uncomfortable position for many people, simply sit up straight so that you are not blocking the flow of energy around your body. Your feet should be firmly on the floor as this will allow any excess or negative energy to flow back to the earth.

Ensure that you are not too hot or too cold, hungry or thirsty as this will distract you when meditating.

This meditation will take around 15 minutes. Do not carry out this meditation if you have to rush off and carry out another task as your mind will not really relax. Instead, your mind will focus on what you have to do rather than what you are actually doing.

Read this section through at least once so that you are familiar with it before you begin. You may wish to ask someone to read it out to you using a calming and soothing voice. Alternatively, you might choose to record these words and play them back to yourself. By following these instructions in this way you will be able to relax quite deeply.

- Begin by closing your eyes.
- Take a deep breath in through your nose and out through your mouth.
- Say to yourself "Relax and let go".
- Find that your body begins to relax a little deeper.
- Now carry on breathing normally.
- Focus your attention on each breath in and out.

(Tip: When you focus your attention on your breathing your mind begins to relax. With your eyes closed your attention is focussed inwardly and less attention is given to outside distractions.)

- As you inhale imagine your lungs being filled with air.
- As you exhale feel yourself relaxing deeper with each out breath.
- Keep breathing in this way for 10 breaths.
- You should now be quite relaxed.
- In order to relax that bit deeper I want you to begin to use your imagination.
- Imagine that you are standing at the top of a beautiful staircase in a lovely large house.
- The steps are safe and secure and there are two sturdy handrails.

- I want you to walk down the steps. I will guide you with each step you take.
  - 10: Begin to step down.
  - 9: Relaxing deeper.
  - 8: Feeling safe.
  - 7: Feeling comfortable.
  - 6: Feeling very, very calm.
  - 5: Floating gently down.
  - 4: Deeper and deeper down.
  - 3: Round and round you go.
  - 2: More deeply relaxed now.
  - 1: Almost there.
  - 0: Now step down, feeling very, very calm and very, very relaxed.

- I want you to imagine that you are now standing facing a door. The door opens out into a beautiful garden.
- Open the door now.
- As you open the door you smell flowers, the garden is very still and quiet. Notice that even if you have allergies you find that those allergies no longer exist and you feel very happy and calm.
- Now step through the door.
- Begin walking in the garden.
- Notice that as you walk your senses take in the fragrance of the flowers, the stillness all around you with the occasional sing song of the birds.

You hear the ocean a short distance away. You feel very, very relaxed now.

- Presently you notice a bench which is overlooking the ocean.
- You decide to sit down.
- As you sit down you notice how very calm and relaxed you feel. You also feel the warmth of the sun on your back and you begin to sink that little bit deeper into a state of very deep relaxation.
- Remember now that this is your time, time just for you where nobody wants or needs anything.
- I want you now to imagine a bright light.
- The light begins at the top of your head.
- Imagine that the light now travels through your body, like a laser beam all the way down to your liver.
- The liver is just under your ribcage on the right hand side.
- Put your hands on your liver and keep them in this position for a couple of minutes.
- Notice any images, emotions, thoughts and feelings that come to mind. Do you feel tired or anxious?
- Does your liver feel heathy?
- When you are ready release any visualisations of the liver.
- Take a deep breath in through your nose and out through your mouth.
- Feel yourself relaxing a little bit deeper.

- Now imagine the light is over your heart.
- I am sure that most of you know where your heart is, but if you are uncertain the heart is located between the lungs and behind the breast bone.
- Once again note any thoughts, feelings and emotions in this area.
- Does your heart feel healthy and strong?
- Does your heart feel empty, sad or full of joy, are you emotionally balanced?
- When you are ready, take a deep breath in through your nose and out through your mouth.
- Now release any visualisations and take a deep breath in through your nose and out through your mouth.
- Relax a little bit deeper once again.
- Once again the light travels through your body.
- This time the light stops at the stomach and the spleen.
- The stomach and the spleen are situated just below the ribcage on the left hand side.
- Place your hands on the stomach and spleen area.
- Now begin to relax a little deeper.
- Make a mental note of any thoughts, feelings or visual imagery that you have. Do you have a healthy stomach? Are you a compassionate person? Can you relate to others and show empathy when necessary?
- When you are ready imagine the light now travelling to your lungs.

- The lungs are located at the sides of the chest.
- Place your hands in this area.
- As you breathe in and out what do you notice? Is your breathing normally smooth and controlled? Are there times when your breathing becomes shallow and slow? Or perhaps you tend to breathe quite quickly? Make a note of any feelings, visualisations or emotions that you experience. Do you have a high level of self- esteem? Please note that your self- esteem refers to your self-worth. How you really value yourself as opposed to how others see and value you.
- When you are ready, breath in deeply then out.
- Relax and let go of any visualisations, thoughts and feelings.
- Finally, allow the light to travel to the kidneys.
- The kidneys are located on either side of the body above the hips.
- Place your hands gently on the kidneys.
- Breathe normally and allow yourself to relax as deeply as possible.
- Once again, focus as deeply as possible and make a mental note of any thoughts, feelings and visualisations that you experience. Ask yourself if you are afraid of anything at the moment. If you are, is that particular thought dominating your life?
- Now I want you take a deep breath in through your nose and out through your mouth.

- In your mind, I want you to stand up from the bench and make your way back through the garden.
- As you walk feel the grass beneath your feet and the sun gently warming your back. You notice that you suddenly feel happy and content and very relaxed.
- Now walk through the door.
- Close the door behind you.
- You are now facing the stairs.
- I want you to begin to walk up the stairs. I will count from 5 to 0 and with each step you take you will become progressively more awake.

  5: Starting to wake up now.

  4: Arms and legs starting to become more awake.

  3: Going up now.

  2: Feeling lighter now.

  1: All of the familiar outside noises are becoming clearer now.

  0: Open your eyes now, fully alert and relaxed.

At this point you might want to make some written notes of what you have thought, felt or even seen during this meditation as you may quickly forget what you have experienced. If this is the first time that you have carried out this meditation you may not have experienced very much as meditation, like most things in life, works best with practice. Try not to be disheartened. Perhaps you may wish to repeat the meditation by focusing on just one or two areas at a time and spending more time on each area.

I hope that this exercise has been useful for you and you have gained some idea of an area(s) of the body that may indicate an imbalance.

The following section explains each of the five elements in detail including the archetypes.

How can I identify my archetype?

As you read the following sections, you will begin to recognise key aspects of your personality. You may also be able to relate to some physical health issues. Please note that you may identify with more than one archetype. This is not uncommon. Archetype/personality traits run through a broad spectrum. If you feel as if you would benefit from carrying out a number of different crystal healing treatments (see below) please do so as these treatments will have an overall positive effect on your health.

Wood

We shall begin our study of each of the individual elements by starting with wood. This element corresponds to the spring. Imagine now that you have rested during the winter and now that spring is here you feel revitalised, energised and very much alive. Spring is the season for developing and renewing friendships and for creating new ones. During this season you have much planning to carry out and you look forward to the future.

If you were to take a walk through the woods during the springtime you would find that the woods have become alive. The sound of the animals, some waking up after hibernating, others newly born and looking at the world with fresh eyes. The woods can appear to be a place of blissful beauty, a little noisy perhaps due to all of this activity. The colour associated with this element is green. If you were, during your walk, to really look at the trees you may find a mixture of old and new. The older trees have become more established and secure, well rooted to the ground. They are safe and know that no matter how much wind, rain and other elements may battle to change their plan of growth, they are here to stay having purpose and direction, although at times they may appear to be a little rigid.

The archetype of the wood element is considered the great thinker, a pioneer even. The sort of person who demonstrates characteristics of the pioneer is one who sets goals and is very focused at achieving them. These people often set up in business themselves after working for someone else as they find that they can do a better job or offer a better service, adding more value to what they do.

The pioneer is a great planner and likes to plan and organise their day to day activities in great depth. If a goal is set and the plan to achieve it is ruined the pioneer takes this very badly. This type of person is sensitive to criticism, very hard working and conscientious and at times critical of others.

The liver is situated in the upper part of the abdomen and connects with the rest of the body through channels. The function of the liver is to remove toxins from the blood and to circulate the blood to the organs of the body and to provide nutrients for the health growth of the nails and hair and to maintain healthy eyes. Just like the branches of a tree that extend far and wide the flow of blood circulates and flows throughout the entire body. Along with the flow of blood the flow of Qi throughout the body is essential to a healthy body, mind and spirit.

A Healthy Balanced Wood Type

- Can see the world objectively.
- Wakes up in the morning with enthusiasm looking forward to the day ahead.
- Is an effective communicator.
- Has a sense of purpose.
- Sets goals and has a vision for the future.
- Is generally creative.
- Can think "outside the box".
- Can be of a sensitive nature.

- Has sparking eyes, windows to a clear vision for the future.
- Has a healthy and balanced diet, this is reflective of a healthy and balanced mind.
- Enjoys walks and gentle exercise.
- Can take on too much leading to frustration at times.
- Has a strong and healthy body

An Imbalanced Wood Type

- Is quick to anger.
- Finds it hard to make decisions.
- Holds onto a grudge.
- Is easily fatigued.
- Suffers frequent headaches, especially on waking.
- Finds it hard to get going.
- Has anxiety.
- Has insomnia and frequent nightmares.
- The liver is also connected to the spleen and when the body is in a high state of imbalance an individual is likely to vomit and have frequent diarrhoea.
- Develops addictions such as alcohol, drugs and overeating.
- Women – menstrual problems.
- Can be overly harsh and critical of others.
- Has no sense of purpose and does not see that it is worth having one.
- Finds day to day tasks more and more difficult to carry out.

- Can develop pain in the chest and the lower stomach as qi is not flowing correctly.
- Is prone to developing muscular skeletal problems. Just as the branches of a tree can become damaged through neglect and age the body can become damaged in the same way if it does not receive what it needs to function correctly.

As the wood type becomes progressively more imbalanced the body begins to deteriorate. In order to help restore good health and vitality a healthy diet is essential with particular emphasis on seasonal green vegetables. Avoid fried and fatty food as these require a lot of work for the liver to digest. Do not eat an excess of dairy products. If anger is one of the main problems then sour foods such as lemons, limes and even vinegar sprinkled over suitable food will help to alleviate the problem. Avoid alcohol if you detect a blockage of energy in the liver or gall bladder. This is because alcohol creates heat and this over stimulates the liver and in this in turn leads to even more anger and negative emotions.

Here is a summary of the element wood. Note, as with all Five Elements, there is a close association to the planets as well as a connection to everything of and within the earth. Qi has no limits, energy travels from our planets to others.

Wood

Planet:	**Jupiter**
Season:	**Spring**
Emotion:	**Anger**
Organ:	**Liver**
Colour:	**Green**

Fire

The fire energy comes from the heart. The season which is associated with this energy is the summer. Think for a few moments about the summer season. What ideas come to mind? Naturally you think about warmth, heat. Think a little deeper – at times the warmth from the sun will burn brightly and then something will appear which will quickly extinguish that warmth. Rain comes and extinguishes the heat leaving you feeling cold, apathetic and lacklustre. Or perhaps the sun goes in behind a cloud and the vitality of the warmth disappears.

The fire types are very similar, when well adapted this type of person attracts others to them by their warm personality, they are fun to be around, kind and considerate, easily able to adapt, the fire type likes to stand out in a crowd. The Fire types tend to live from the heart and this is home of the Shen or spirit. The Shen lives in all of the organs but especially in the heart. The colour which is associated with the heart is red. This is the colour of love, passion and intimacy. When the energy from the fire archetype is strong this type of person has limitless love for those closest to them and compassion and love for all of humanity. Although they like to take control, it is in the area of relationships that they really seek power. If you become observant and begin to notice the archetypes which are present in your life, when you next notice a fire type you will observe that they like to take control of conversations and at times they will even be seen to finish other people sentences off for them in order to take control or command of their environment.

The fire element consists of the heart, the small intestine, the circulatory system and the autonomic nervous system (both sympathetic and parasympathetic branches). In traditional Chinese medicine, the small intestine controls the mind and the sympathetic nervous system protects the heart, making the person strong emotionally and rendering the person less emotionally vulnerable. When an imbalance occurs the fire archetype is likely to experience cardiovascular problems, high or low blood pressure, often they become shy, depressed and retire from social contacts as they lose their ability to connect with others.

The archetype for the fire element is the wizard. Being able to hold his audience spell bound with exciting and meaningful tales the wizard attracts people to him and is warm and friendly to approach. I am sure we all know someone like this. A person who people seem to be attracted to like a magnet who is able to offer advice and just seems to know what to do and what to say. Perhaps this is you?

A Healthy Balanced Fire Type

- Has a good sense of humour.
- Enjoys the company of other people.
- Attracts friends easily.
- Has the ability to laugh at themselves.
- Is considered to be an optimistic person.
- Is confident in almost any situation.
- Has a sense of drive and purpose in life.
- Enjoys taking control of situations.
- Has the capacity to love deeply and to develop very deep loving relationships.
- Enjoys helping others.
- Has a strong and healthy heart and cardiovascular system.
- Enjoys playful and creative activities.

An Imbalanced Fire Type

- Often shows commitment to a task but this quickly burns out.
- Makes poor judgements and decisions.
- Lacks passion and enthusiasm
- Avoids social situations whenever possible.
- On the occasions when social interaction is necessary, they seek out other similar, fire types to help to re-kindle their energy.
- Develops heart problems.
- Finds life difficult to cope with and often feels under pressure.
- Feels vulnerable.
- Feels anxious most of the time.
- Lacks the ability to love and be intimate.

Fire

Planet: **Mars**

Season: **Summer**

Emotion: **Happiness**

Organ: **The heart**

Colour: **Red**

Earth

The earth element allows us to feel connected and abundant. Most of us are familiar with someone like this. The selfless giving, nurturing and unconditional love and support are at the core of all that the earth types do.

The earth archetype is the Peacemaker. When balanced the earth archetypes are the sort of people who are the first to welcome newcomers into the neighbourhood, they are also the first to offer help to those in need, tend to the sick and organise support groups when needed. Because of their warm and loving nature earth types tend to attract people who have problems that need solving. They are non-judgemental and supportive to family, friends and even strangers if the need arises. They are the hub of any community.

The organs that the earth types are associated with are the stomach and the spleen. Interestingly, these are the organs that help to digest and assimilate food, breaking down food so that it is converted into Qi for the body to utilise. The stomach and the spleen are involved in the digestive process, taking food from the earth, breaking it down, transforming it into energy starting at the mouth with mastication.

The colour of the earth element is yellow, a beautiful colour full of optimism and hope for the future. The season that is associated with the earth element is late summer. During the late summer we often think about the changes ahead, depending on where we live we may have to plan for winter and the colder weather. Late summer is a time for planning, thinking, respecting and appreciating the earth and all that she has to offer.

When an earth type becomes maladapted they will often become harsh and critical and selfish. Less willing to do for others they often become self-absorbed and this change in behaviour pushes people away leading, at times, to social isolation which then becomes a vicious cycle, as less social contact leads to greater maladapted behaviour. On the other hand the earth type may become smothering, obsessive and overbearing. Willing to give and offer to others to the detriment of their own health and financial security, the earth types can often be seen as martyrs when maladapted.

A Healthy Balanced Earth Type

- Is willing to help others at their time of need.
- Offers useful and non-judgemental advice.
- Is compassionate.
- Has empathy.
- Is a doer.
- Has energy and drive.
- Enjoys helping and serving others.
- Focuses on solutions and not problems.

A Maladapted Earth Type

- Over mothers.
- Becomes obsessive.
- Becomes withdrawn and selfish.
- Craves sugar.
- Lacks empathy – harsh and uncaring.
- Worries constantly.
- Have stomach and digestive problems.
- May develop diabetes.

Earth	
Planet:	**Saturn**
Season:	**Late Summer**
Organ:	**Stomach**
Emotion:	**Empathy/love**
Colour:	**Yellow**

Metal

Autumn is the season that is associated with the metal type. Leaves fall from the trees, often becoming crisp and colourful. There is a sense of expectation, anticipation and reflection in the air. What will the following weeks bring? Fruit begins to decay, darkness begins to set in. There is a physical slowing down in preparation for winter.

The alchemist is the archetype that is associated with metal. The alchemist is able to quietly restore order to a chaotic environment, able to sort out what is needed and worthwhile in order to get the job done. The alchemist is not so much interested in material goods but rather the true value of a person is determined by their behaviour and actions rather than what they say and have. The alchemist establishes their own set of values from what they have learnt from their father. A heavenly father is one who knows all, one to be treated with respect and who in turn must be seen to be fair, offer unconditional love and most of all treat the child with respect. This is fundamental to the metal type. If respect is not given the child will develop low self-esteem, as an adult they will seek the affirmation and respect of others in order to feel loved. If a child is not fortunate enough to have a parent who is capable of treating the child well, as long as a father figure is present in the child's life the metal type will thrive.

I am sure you know many metal types in your life. They are the sort of people who will do not engage in gossip and bad mouth others. They are able to take in all of the facts when establishing wrong doing. Often seen as solid in character, dependable and trustworthy, they live by their own set of high morals and values and often find it difficult to understand when others do not seem capable of following their "code". Because of this, metal types often appear to be a little aloof and apart from other people.

Metal types thrive well in jobs that require objectivity, the legal profession, science and medicine are all great areas for metal types to work in as they are mostly working with factual information. The autumn season represents change and loss. As the darkness of the season sets in, so can the darkness of grief and loss. Metal types can be prone to holding onto the emotion of grief. Letting go of grief and letting go and relaxing are difficult for the metal types. Just as a tree will let go of its leaves in autumn when they are no longer needed, the metal types must learn to let go of grief in order to be able to function healthily. Maladapted metal types prefer to work on their own as they feel that others are not able to do the job as well as they can. They often hold grudges, become harsh in their words with others and are generally unhappy with their lives and with others around them.

The organs which correspond to the metal element are the lungs and the colon. The lungs take in the air from the earth and the inspiration from the heavens. The colon is involved in sorting out and extracting. Waste products are removed and this process is also involved in removing and extracting grief and loss and allowing the process of emotional healing to begin. The lungs, taking in air, bring in hope and inspiration for life.

A Well Adapted Metal Type

- A strong moral code.
- High self-esteem.
- Is able to get the job done in a calm manner.
- Does not excessively pursue material goods.
- Can be flexible if the situation requires it.
- Values other people.

A Maladapted Metal Type

- Prefers to work alone.
- Can be very critical of self and others.
- Holds grudges.
- Is unreliable.
- Health problems: including headaches, congestion, sore throats, backache, frozen shoulder and irritable bowel syndrome.

Metal

Planet:	**Venus**
Season:	**Autumn**
Emotion:	**Grief**

Organs: **Lungs and colon**

Colour: **White/Silver**

Water

Water, essential to life, is the element that is associated with the kidneys and bladder as both are involved in the urinary process. The water element represents knowledge and the capacity and willingness to learn more by its ability to travel and to reach out in all directions. Winter is the season associated with the water element and the Chinese associate it with colours of dark purple and black. Winter represents stillness and death, knowledge and experience and the ability to move on to the next stage.

The water archetype is the Sage or Philosopher – full of knowledge and wisdom the water types always want to know more. Jing DNA from the kidneys contains genetic material, knowledge and wisdom which can be passed through the generations. These types are clever, great at observing, patient and wise. Imagine a grandparent who listens to you without judging, has empathy and understanding but is still firm and willing to put you on the right track. Some water types are outgoing and fun to be around, others are much more serious and a little shy. All water types are interested in conserving energy from the kidneys. Some will work until they are burnt out and then rest whilst others are happy working at a steady pace and conserving energy whenever possible.

When imbalanced the Philospher will lack energy and loses interest in projects. Fear is the emotion that is associated with this archetype. Fear of growing old and fear of the unknown are common. Although to some degree, fear prevents reckless behaviour and keeps us safe whilst overwhelming, fear which is felt in the chest, prevents a person from moving forward and progressing in life. As we grow older we find that kidney Jing declines with age. We may become too cold or too hot, become menopausal or develop urinary problems such as incontinence.

A Balanced Water Type

- Is patient and wise.
- Has intelligence.
- Demonstrates a willingness to learn.
- Is a good listener.
- Is committed to projects and goals.
- Is willing to accept the unknown and the unexpected.

An Imbalanced Water Type

- Is fearful, even phobic if very imbalanced.
- Inpatient.
- Unable to adapt.

- Unwilling to compromise.
- Rigid thought patterns.
- Often feels overwhelmed.
- Often feels isolated.

Water

Planet:	**Mercury**
Season:	**Winter**
Emotion:	**Fear**
Organ:	**Kidneys/Bladder**
Colour:	**Dark purple/Black**

AN INTRODUCTION
TO CRYSTALS

From when time began humans have always been interested in crystals, gemstones and rocks. In science fiction movies strange and unusual stones have been considered to be a source of power, often forcing the bearer of the crystal to change their behaviour, a form of mind control. These days crystals can be used to make changes: to support health and well-being, to act as an attractive piece of jewellery, used in computers or to add energy and vitality to a room by removing negative vibrations.

So, what actually are crystals and where do they come from? The word crystal is often used by healers to include any small stones. Tumble stones for example are often used to aid healing and these small stones are called crystals. To be factually correct here, a crystal must have specific properties in order to be, well, called a crystal. Importantly a crystal must have a solid body which forms a crystal lattice and is composed of a complex mixture of atoms, protons and ions.

Crystals have their unique shape due to the environment in which they are formed. If you were to break a crystal into many small parts and look at it under a microscope you will find that each crystal is identical to the other small crystals in shape and that shape is the same as the large crystal which you had just broken. Crystals are found in 7 different shapes; however, there are of course exceptions to every rule and some beautiful crystals have been discovered which have their own very unique shape.

Crystals are not always found where they are formed or formed where they are found. Sometimes minerals are formed deep the earth itself and moved by natural activity such as volcanic activity. In other situations mining can bring the minerals to the earth surface. Water near the earth's surface interacts with the minerals and dissolves them. It is the chemical composition of the solution that changes the minerals that ultimately decides what form the crystal takes. Water combined with silica will produce agate for example.

Crystals can be found in many countries in the world, however to begin with you might want to think a little closer to home. Table salt is composed of the mineral sodium chloride, found in nearly every home it is often an ingredient in processed foods and is used in cooking. Unfortunately salt has gained a bad reputation and this is because table salt has most of the helpful properties removed during manufacturing. Sea salt, however, in small amounts can be very beneficial to health. Amongst the advantages are that sea salt can help to remove toxins from the body, boron found in sea salt can help to prevent osteoporosis and chromium, also found in sea salt, can help to regulate blood sugar levels and actually lower blood pressure. Naturally I am talking about the use of very small amounts of sea salt here and if any of my readers wish to know how to use sea salt to support any nutritional programme they wish to follow, it is advisable that they consult their health care professionals who will be able to offer further advice as sea salt may be toxic in large amounts.

One of the largest discoveries of crystals was found in the year 2000 in Chihuahua, Mexico. Two brothers mining came across some of the largest selenite crystals every discovered. The crystals are said to be 500,000 years old and although the cave is not open to the general public at this moment in time, some of the crystals are said to be at least 10m long.

A rare crystal called Putnisite, measuring only half a millimetre in diameter and usually found in Australia, has now been discovered in Vanuatu in the South Pacific. It is thought that the crystals were transported via volcanic activity to the island. The discovery of crystals on the island has led some scientists to re-evaluate how it was possible for crystals to reach this location as it was previously thought that the island, east of Australia, had been isolated from the continent. Scientists are looking to carry out further studies in this area.

Throughout the world crystals and gemstones can be found in abundance. Citrine, which is a brown/red variety of quartz, for example, can be found in Brazil, Congo, Russia, France and Spain. Citrine is commonly formed by heat treating purple amethyst.

Throughout the world you will find crystals and gemstones that can be used to help you heal on so many levels. As you can see, further locations are being discovered all of the time. I wonder where the next big discovery will be?

As you progress through this book you will discover where in your body you are out of balance (if anywhere) and what crystals you can use to correct this imbalance. Before you begin I will provide you with a little background information so that you will know how to:

- Select your crystals
- Where to buy them
- How to cleanse them

How to Select Your Crystals
Earlier today I was chatting with a colleague who informed me that she had purchased some crystals

online and when she received her order she discovered that they were of very poor quality indeed and that some were unfortunately damaged. The online supplier denied liability and my friend has now lost quite a large amount of money. I mention this, not because I do not approve of online shops or traders. Quite the opposite in fact as I have purchased many quality crystals online. At times, depending on the crystal that you wish to buy, an online purchase may be the only option. I write about this incident to inform you that not all crystals of the same name are of equal quality and not all sellers are totally honest about the product that they are selling. So, how can you minimise the risk of buying a faulty or inferior product?

Where to Buy Crystals

Purchasing crystals online: Research the company that is selling the crystals, search for reviews, if everything seems to be in order make a small purchase first, in that way you are able to establish if the company offers a professional and timely service and if they offer quality products. At times a product may arrive damaged through insufficient packaging or poor handing from the postal company. Bear in mind that this may be a one off and it is with the efficiency and speed that the product is replaced or refunded that you need to consider when assessing the worthiness and integrity of the seller.

Purchasing crystals at a fair or special event: This is a great way for you to purchase a crystal as you are able to handle it and evaluate the quality of the stone before buying. Unfortunately, many people have probably done the same, and this has left the stone with a lot of negative energy which can change its vibrational frequency. If you purchase crystals in this way please read the section on how to cleanse them carefully.

Purchasing crystals from a crystal shop: I absolutely love crystal shops! Just walking through the door leaves me feeling instantly energised and uplifted. The problem is that it is often difficult to get me out of the shop because I become so drawn to so many of the crystals that I feel compelled to picking them up, feeling their vibrations and energy. Often these shops are managed and run by wonderful staff who are very knowledgeable and are aware of the potential healing properties of the stones, as well as where you may be able to locate crystals in your area. Perhaps you need a unique crystal and have difficulty locating it; the staff at the shop may be able to order it in for you.

When you buy crystals from a specific shop the crystal may have been on the shelf for a while. There may be dust on it and, just like when buying from events and fairs, the crystal may have been handled many times before you decided to purchase it. Remember that you will need to give the crystal a deep clean when you get it home and that it may feel slightly different as the vibrational frequency may have changed a little as negative energy will be released during the cleaning process.

Choosing crystals using your intuition: I really enjoy buying crystals simply because I am drawn to them! Sometimes it is as if I am hypnotised and feel compelled to buy a specific stone. I may not know why I am buying it, but I trust that the reason for making the purchase will become apparent over time.

There may be times that you buy a crystal without really knowing the properties of it. It is only later that you discover that something is out of balance within your body and that the crystal is used to help you to heal. Coral, sapphire and emerald tumble stones for example are used to lift depression. Do you carry any of these small stones around with you but do not really know why?

A crystal gift: If someone gives you a gift of a crystal either in the form of a set of crystals, an individual one or a piece of jewellery a question is often asked will the crystal work for me? The answer to that question is yes. This is because most people are quite intuitive and seem to know, without even thinking too much about it, exactly what to purchase. Often people are drawn to a specific coloured stone and feel that it is just right for the intended recipient. This may be because it is their favourite colour and strangely that is the correct coloured stone that can be used to help to heal a person either mentally, physically and emotionally.

There may be times when the vibrations of a crystal do not feel quite right. The vibrations may feel too quick, leading to feelings of dizziness and nausea, or too slow, leading to feelings of being very heavy and being pulled to the ground. I remember that I once purchased a beautiful citrine necklace as I was very drawn to it at a fair. When I held the necklace and tried it on it appeared to be fine. I took it home and, being conscious that many people had handled it, I cleansed it by leaving it overnight in a bowl of clear water. The next time I put the necklace on I immediately felt sick and dizzy and when I removed the necklace I felt fine once more. I cleansed the necklace again and placed it by the window, with good sunlight but not where it would get too much heat. A few days later I placed the necklace around my neck and waited. I felt fine. I waited for a few minutes more. Yes I felt fine. I was able to wear the necklace and I am still able to wear it.

What was the reason for the uncomfortably fast vibrations that I had felt? There are two possibilities: firstly, as crystals are living stones that particular citrine stone may not have felt in line with my vibrational frequency at that time. I then reflected on how I was feeling at the time that I first wore the necklace and I remembered that I had been feeling quite highly energised.

Citrine helps to create a sense of confidence whilst lifting low self-esteem. Citrine also helps to eliminate thyroid problems, kidney and bladder problems and any problems associated with the spleen and the pancreas. I believe that I was on a very high vibrational frequency. The happier and more confident you are, the higher your vibrational frequency and those with a lower vibrational frequency tend to feel unhappy or even depressed. As I was functioning at such a high level of vibrational frequency, the citrine in the necklace was not needed to help and support me. The result was my feelings of sickness and dizziness. It was almost as if the citrine was telling me – hey I am not needed here at this moment in time. The second possibility that I have thought of is that the citrine had not been cleansed sufficiently. It is important to cleanse crystals for up to twenty four hours when you first get them. It is possible that this particular stone needed more and after a second cleanse and placing the necklace where it was close to natural sunlight, which is energising, the crystal was able to adjust to the correct vibrational frequency with time. As you can see, working with crystals and energy is a very personal experience. Understanding your body and any potential imbalances is also difficult. This all takes time and do not become disillusioned if you are new to this type of work.

How to Cleanse Your Crystals

There are a number of ways in which you can do this. Please remember that it is very important to ensure that you clean your crystals on a regular basis. Dust and the odd particle of dirt will naturally accumulate over time, this will leave the crystals losing their sparkle and they will not be able to function effectively. In addition, you need to be able to "connect" with your crystal and what better way to bond with it than to nurture and care for it than by cleaning it? A crystal is like a plant, it needs love and attention.

Quick Ways to clean your crystals

Running water: Simply turn on the tap and allow the crystals to be cleansed by running, cold tap water. Allow the tap to run for around 30 minutes.

Bury your crystals: Bury your crystals in the earth in a place that you feel drawn to. Make sure that it is a familiar place and one that you will remember or else you may have problems finding your crystal(s) again.

Water & Salt: Add half a mug of salt to a bowl of water and stir to allow an even distribution. Place your crystals in the bowl and leave overnight. In the morning, gently take the crystals out of the bowl and place under running water for thirty minutes. This is a great way to ensure that crystals which have not been cleansed for a while receive a deep clean and it only take a few minutes of your time!

Salt: Use sea salt if you have it or table salt if this is more readily available in your home. Fill a bowl with salt and place your crystal in it. Leave the crystal in the bowl overnight. There is no need to wash them with water as the sea salt or table salt is very purifying, will cleanse deeply and the particles of salt will not attach themselves to the crystal and so will not need to be washed away.

Please remember to throw away the salt afterwards. The salt will have absorbed a lot of negative energy and I am sure that you will not want to ingest all of this negativity by using the salt in your cooking or on food. You should not keep the salt and think of using it at some other point in the future when you may wish to cleanse your crystals again as the salt will have a lot of negative energy and this may affect the crystals delicate vibrations, in addition to not cleansing the crystals properly anyway. The only use I can think of for the salt that you have used for your crystals is this- if it is winter and you live in a cold climate and it is icy you may wish to throw the salt on your path to help the ice melt.

Important: It is not advisable for you to cleanse all crystals in salt as the salt can change the shape and even the properties of them. Some of the crystals which should never be cleansed in this manner are:

- Opals
- Lapis lazuli
- Pyrite

If in doubt, leave salt out and simply wipe the crystals with a wet cloth and gently dry afterwards, I find this method works best with mine.

Moon light: Leave your crystals out during a full moon. The magical properties of a full moon will leave your crystals full of energy and sparkling, ready to do what it does best – emit a lovely vibration.

Smudging: You will need a little time for this. Burn a smudge stick and pass it over the crystal. The crystal will let go of any negativity that it is holding onto. When I do this I am always surprised at how much lighter and generally different the crystal feels.

Now that you have the very basics on how to select, buy and clean your crystals you can move forward and find out what crystals work best with each of the Five Elements and how you can use them.

CRYSTALS FOR HEALING

In this next section you will be introduced to crystals which are especially known to have specific healing properties. I have carefully selected ten crystals for each of the five archetypes associated with the Five Elements. Before you discover what those crystals are, I want to introduce you to other ways in which you can use them. You may choose to use only one crystal, more than one or purchase all ten of the crystals listed in any one category in order to make the most of the combined healing potential of the crystals. It is your choice and there really is no right or wrong. Use your intuition to guide you.

Wearing crystals as jewellery

You may wish to wear your crystals as jewellery. I find that wearing a crystal necklace especially one that lies over the throat or the heart has many healing benefits. A word of caution, if you feel tired or overwhelmed when wearing your crystal jewellery, remove the item from your person and cleanse it using any of the methods mentioned in the previous chapter.

Carry your crystal(s) in your pocket or in a pouch

Some people prefer to carry their crystals. This could be because they do not like wearing jewellery or that they may not be able to find jewellery that they like bearing that particular crystal. Often men do not like wearing crystal jewellery. I advise them to wear their crystal on a chain under a shirt or similar. In this way they are receiving the healing benefits of the crystal without feeling uncomfortable that they may be drawing attention to wearing what they may perceive as ladies jewellery. If you choose to carry your crystal in your pocket please be careful to ensure that it will not be scratched by anything else that you carry in the same pocket such as coins or keys. If you carry more than one crystal in the same pocket the same might happen. In order to prevent this from happening many people choose to carry their crystals around in a small velvet pouch. Simply pop your crystal into the pouch and slip it into your pocket. You can carry several crystals in this way and they will not scratch each other.

Using crystals as decorations

Some people choose to decorate their homes or particular rooms in their home using crystals. I have a room that I use for healing. In this room I have crystals on a shelf, in the window and a couple hanging from the ceiling.

My healing room is my favourite room in my home as is always full of energy and if I am feeling tired or a little down I always go straight to my healing room, because in a matter of minutes I am feeling great once again.

Crystal balls are also wonderful tools to energise a room. Place four crystal balls, one in each corner of the room. The energy and vibrations from each individual crystal ball will expand, fill and uplift the room. This will amplify the energy, as energy from one ball connects with the other. Alternatively, if the layout of the room is not suitable for four crystal balls, place one single crystal ball in a place where it will attract the light. The crystal will thank you and use its energy to fill the room. Crystal balls attract dust – please remember to gently wipe over the crystal ball on a regular basis as part of your cleaning routine. In addition, remember to clean it in salt when the ball looks tired or dull or if there has been a lot of negative energy in the room. The best way to cleanse a crystal ball is to soak it in salt overnight. Gently remove any excess salt particles by rubbing the ball with a clean, dry cloth afterwards. Clear quartz and rose quartz are the most commonly used types of crystal balls that individuals use for decorative purposes.

Crystal wands can also be used. You can use the same layout as mentioned above. Howlite is commonly used for calming someone, or to support a relaxing environment and black obsidian, which helps to remove psychic confusion and aid mental clarity, is also very popular. I have just purchased a lovely serpentine wand. This wand has lovely calming and healing properties and is often said to be the healer's crystal.

Vogel wands have lovely healing potential. A vogel wand is a quartz crystal wand that has been cut in a specific way. The wands are named after the research scientist, Marcel Vogel (1917 to 1991) who worked for IBM and was interested in the study of light. The wands must be cut in such a way as to collect, amplify and transmit light. The small wands can retail at around thirty dollars (US).Those wands that are purchased from one of the few people who were trained in the specific cutting application and technique used by Marcel Vogel are much more expensive retailing at several hundred dollars for a small one.

Using crystals in the home

In the bath . When you run a bath simply place your crystals in the running water. Minerals from the crystals will dissolve in the water and you will receive the healing benefits when you have a bath. You could use your favourite bath essence as this will not affect the minerals in the water in any way or you may choose to simply place several crystals into the bath and have a lovely bath using natural resources, crystals and water. This is a great way to cleanse your aura too.

Under your pillow. If you have problems sleeping you might want to place some celestite or amethyst under your pillow. These stones will calm the mind and aid relaxation and a deep sleep.

Crystals around your work place. If your workplace is a little negative and you feel as if there are energy vampires sucking all of the life and soul from the environment, place some labradorite, rose quartz or amber on your desk or anywhere else which is a suitable environment. Try it and see what happens.

In your car. Driving used to be such a pleasurable experience. Now we all seem to want or need to get from A to B in the blink of an eye. Try placing some green aventurine or strawberry quartz to help keep you calm, focused on the moment and relaxed when driving.

How can crystals help me heal?

Our human bodies are made up of vibrations. Indeed, all living creatures including plants down to the smallest, the amoeba, a tiny organism made up of just one cell, all contain vibrations. Our vibrations change all of the time depending on how we feel. The way we feel not only depends on our emotions at any particular time but on our metabolism and the chemical reactions that occur within the body. The chemical reactions that occur depend on our thoughts and feelings. As you can see, our vibrations are dependent on our physical and emotional state at any one time.

All around the body there is an aura. The aura is not one but several layers. Each layer is connected to the body by the skin. The layers of the aura which are the closest to the body have fairly low and dense vibrations and the further away from the physical body you go the vibrations are higher/more rapid.

When carrying out any healing treatment, and in this category I include Reiki, the more experienced and sensitive an individual is to the energy the more they will be able to feel the different types of vibrations. At times the vibrations are quite slow and dense and at other times very rapid, almost as if you are placing your hands on a washing machine as it goes into a spin cycle. For myself, when the vibrations are like this I have to ensure that I am well grounded. By this I mean that I make sure that my feet are on the ground, bare feet if possible, so that the excess energy caused by the vibrations has the chance to go back to the earth and become re-cycled into the atmosphere.

When you first begin to use any crystals it is a good idea to become familiar with them. Make your crystals your friends by understanding them! This may sound a little strange, so why not carry out the following exercise to see what I mean:

Read this exercise through before carrying it out so that you will fully understand what to do.

- Find somewhere quiet where you will not be disturbed. Avoid sitting near electronic devices, and this naturally includes your mobile phone.
- Place a crystal near to you (only use one at a time).
- Turn the palms of your hands upwards.
- Notice any gentle tingling sensations or if you feel drawn to using one hand in particular. Most of us have one hand that is much more sensitive to energy and vibrations that the other. If you are completely new to this type of work it may take you several attempts to establish which hand is your sensitive hand and which is not. If you are struggling, try this exercise with one hand this time and with the other hand on another occasion. Don't worry, with time your degree of sensitivity will develop.
- Place the crystal in the palm of your hand.
- Close your eyes. It is important to do this because when your eyes are closed you are reducing the level of stimulation you receive from your visual sense. This will allow your senses to focus more on what you are feeling.
- And now wait.

Leave the crystal in the palm of your hand for several minutes. During this time you may feel a gentle tingling sensation, buzzing, vibrating, pulling, heaviness, lightness, oh so many things! What you are experiencing are the crystals individual vibrations. If you feel any discomfort it is because the crystal is vibrating either too quickly or too slowly for you. Imagine that you are talking to another person. The person is, say excitable and talking quickly and you, on the other hand, are feeling calm and relaxed and talking much more slowly. Even though you are both talking the same language your speech is not aligned with theirs and some adjustment has to be made. Either you begin to talk quickly or they begin to talk slowly. When you are both at the same level, balance will be restored.

With crystals, each crystal has its own specific vibrational frequency. Each type of crystal will have a similar vibrational frequency to others of the same type. This is how we know which crystals can be used to help support the healing process with each condition. When holding a crystal in the palm of your hand your vibrations from your energy system at that particular time will interact with the vibrations of the crystals and this is how the healing process is supported.

Now there are times when a particular crystal may make you feel uncomfortable. This may be because the energy from that crystal is too strong or the vibrations are too fast or too slow. When this happens, cleanse the crystal using any of the methods mentioned elsewhere in this book and try using the crystal again. If the same thing happens it is likely that the crystal does not wish to work with you at this time. Use the crystal as a decoration in the home or if it is a piece of jewellery hang it where it can receive gentle sunlight. Weeks or even months later try using the crystal again, cleanse prior to using and see what happens.

It is possible that the crystal had a strong build-up of energy which had to be gradually released and once released the crystal is able to adjust to its correct vibrational frequency. On the other hand the vibrations from your energy field could have been too quick or to slow depending on the state of your health at the time you tried to use the crystal. Now, more adjusted and aligned, you and your crystal can work well together.

When using crystals in your home as decorations, in the car or workplace, the crystals will emit their vibrations into the atmosphere therefore energising it and helping to remove negative energy. Just like any decoration within the home, a crystal needs to be dusted, cleansed and taken care of.

When using crystals for healing on the body a number of layouts can be used and as you progress through this section you will be introduced to some of them. Crystals will help to remove negative energy from the body during healing. It is this negative energy which has built up over time and become toxic leading to dis-ease.

Crystals can be expensive to buy and my advice here is to purchase a few at a time to build up your collection. Crystal quartz are great healing crystals to begin your collection. These lovely stones will amplify their energy outwards. I would suggest that you purchase several crystal quartz stones, along with one or two of the healing crystals from the archetype that you are interested in re-balancing. This is a good way to begin and you can buy other crystals as and when you are able to.

Important – please read the section below before continuing

For each of the five elements I have detailed a crystal healing treatment that is based on the position of the meridians. These are energy pathways through which energy flows when healthy and can become blocked and stagnant when unwell.

From experience, as I have carried out many crystal healing treatments, some with and some without Reiki and I have discovered that the positions of the crystals detailed below and throughout this book are likely to produce the best results.

How long does the treatment last?

To begin with, a treatment should last between 15 and 30 minutes. If you feel uncomfortable in any way you can either remove the crystal(s) that is causing you to feel discomfort or you can stop the treatment altogether. I have only once had to stop a crystal treatment because of this as the client was very sensitive. I use the term "client" throughout this session as this is the word that I use to treat clients, family and friends.

I would not recommend that you continue a treatment beyond the recommended time period. Do not underestimate the healing potential of the crystals and go beyond that time, especially at first. The energy from the crystals can be very subtle and you may not feel it at first resulting in a mistaken belief that the treatment is not working or that you need to carry on with the treatment longer than suggested.

In my clinic my sessions last for 50 minutes. If a client is having a crystal treatment, then the first treatment is carried out for the recommended time period and the rest of the treatment comprises of a Reiki session. Gradually, and usually over a course of 6 sessions I increase the time of the crystal healing session by 5 minutes until all of the 50 minute session is taken up with crystal healing. I often enhance the power of the crystals by adding Reiki healing as well, resulting in a quite powerful treatment.

It is wise to check on the client after around 10 minutes of crystal healing. This is to ensure that all is well. Often, due to the stillness and healing atmosphere, the client will be asleep. Although only a few crystals are generally placed on the client's body, it is a good idea to check to see if those crystals have fallen off. If they have **do not replace them**. The crystals could have fallen off due to poor positioning or perhaps the crystal energy is too strong and not suitable for the client at this time. Simply keep a note of this.

When the session has ended, remove the crystals one at a time, in the order in which they were placed. Allow the client a few minutes to become fully awake. A drink of water is usually much appreciated at this time. Note any comments or observations that the client makes as this could offer some insight into how the body has become imbalanced in the first place. Armed with this, the client could then take the necessary steps to support improved health by making lifestyle changes. A client, for example, might have a dream or experience during the session that will indicate that they need to change job, make relationship changes or something else. These changes are not always easy and additional support in the form of counselling or psychotherapy may be needed by a suitably qualified person in order to facilitate these changes.

Not everyone needs to make drastic changes in order to support and restore good health and well-being. Many people simply end up working too hard, take on too much and become over tired and burdened with life. For the majority a quick review of how they manage their time and a little rest will be enough along with a few crystal healing treatments to help finely balance the body. Health and vitality will then be restored.

How long apart should I carry out the treatments?

To begin with: 2 sessions per week for 3 weeks then weekly thereafter if required.

How many sessions will I need in total?

I usually suggest 6 sessions. Some people will need more, some less depending on the problem as each person is an individual.

Why are some crystals listed in more than one section?
Nearly all crystals have more than one use and I have tried to list the best one in order for the treatment to be the most effective.

Does each crystal have a specific position?
No. The crystals will work together. Simply follow the suggested layout and place individual crystals in the suggested positions but there is no specific position for say, Rose Quartz. The combined energy from the crystals will help support the healing process.

Wood

The archetype of the wood element is the pioneer. The pioneer is creative and when well-balanced sets goals and achieves them. At times the pioneer can be aggressive, argumentative and totally fixated on achieving his goals. As in most things in life, balance is the key. When the pioneer archetype becomes too controlling he is also out of balance and must learn to restore his compassion and patience with others. Equally, when the pioneer lacks vision and drive he must seek to restore balance within. Anger is a common emotion experienced by the pioneer. When he is angry the anger rises upwards throughout the body and this causes the energy to become imbalanced.

Useful Crystals

Moss Agate

This lovely green stone is combined with other minerals which results in the stone looking like green moss. The energy from the stone results in in being a very powerful emotional healing stone as well as helping to aid your concentration. This is an excellent benefit for the pioneer archetype as this type of person needs a high level of concentration in order to achieve the goals he sets himself. Use this stone if you feel that you need greater mental clarity and additional support in goal setting and achieving.

Moonstone

This stone will help the user delve deep into themselves and discover what they truly want to do and achieve in life. The stone will help the user discover what it is they need to do and give them the support and courage in order to work towards their goals.

Green Aventurine

This stone, of the Quartz family, can be used to help the pioneer archetype become even tempered and calm. The user of this stone will begin to slow down a little and appreciate nature more. When a person slows down a little, they are able to see more clearly what is going on around them. This stone is great for drawing out and seeing the opportunities for development that are all around us.

Alabaster

This is mostly a white stone which often comes with a hint of other colours depending on where it has been found and what other minerals it has combined with. Alabaster is a drawing stone – it is used to draw the answer to your questions to you and to draw things that do not serve you away from you. This is a good stone for the pioneer to use as it will help him to draw the answer that is right for him to any dilemma and to draw away any negativity.

Green Jade

Many crystals are sold as jade, but real Jade is found from one of two minerals:

Jadeite – made from sodium aluminium silicate.

Nephrite – calcium magnesium iron silicate.

Jade can be used to help the pioneer archetype achieve greater wealth and prosperity. The immune system and the eyes are also supported when this stone is used. The pioneer also has a heightened sense of justice and Jade helps to draw a sense of equality and balance to all that the pioneer does and is attracted to achieving. Often pioneer archetypes are concerned with good causes and helping the vulnerable and this stone will help support them in their work.

Agate

This stone is found from volcanic rock and is able to keep the pioneer archetype feeling calm in the presence of adversity. Agate used to be worn by warriors to promote courage and good luck in times of battle.

Rose Quartz

This lovely stone from the quartz family can be used to help the user feel love and compassion. The stone can be used to help ease rejection and I have included it in this section because it is an ideal stone to help support the pioneer archetype when he is feeling rejected or when things have not gone very well for him. Remember that the pioneer is very goal focused and when those goals are not achieved, for whatever reason, the pioneer can become very disheartened. Healing derived from rose quartz can help combat those negative feelings and restore emotional balance once again.

Crystal Quartz

This stone can be used to remove negative energy caused by your own negative thoughts and feelings and those caused by others. This stone can help the pioneer archetype think with greater clarity and is a great aid to emotional stability as well as promoting emotional strength.

Fluorite

This is a wonderful crystal to help protect the user from psychic attack, which often comes in the form of negative comments from other people. Negative energy can help discourage the pioneer from achieving his goals, especially if he is feeling a little uncertain and apprehensive. We all encounter people like this; people who tell us that we cannot, or will not, achieve our vision. Fluorite will also help the user feel more at peace, creating higher self-esteem and with that a greater ability to look objectively at what they wish to achieve.

Malachite

This stone helps the physical body by supporting the

liver and the immune system. The pioneer archetype is highly prone to stress, this in turn affects the immune system and results in mild physical illness at first resulting in other immune system disorders as the stress continues. Malachite helps to promote a sense of balance within the physical body of the user as well as promoting a sense of inner calm and tranquillity.

A crystal treatment to help balance energy flowing through the liver

Crystals needed: 12

As I have suggested previously, it may be wise to purchase a number of clear quartz crystals as these are great for healing as well as one or two of the specific crystals mentioned above. Ideally, you need someone to help you position the crystals as it may be a little tricky trying to do this yourself. You will need to lie flat on a bed or a couch and keep your arms and legs slightly apart from your body.

You need to ensure that you are comfortable, that the room is warm and that you will not be disturbed. Remember that this is your time and that you deserve some quality time to yourself.

Place the crystals in the following order:

- Start at the big toe – place one crystal at the heel of each foot in line with your big toe.
- One on the inside of each knee.
- One between the top of the legs.
- One on the stomach area.
- Right side – use two crystals over the liver area. Remember, the liver is positioned on the right side of the abdomen and under the diaphragm.
- One on the throat.
- At the top of the head (but not on the head itself).
- One each side of the eyes.

For treatment duration and further information please see the section above.

Fire

Fire energy is connected to the heart. The spirit or the Shen lies within all organs, but the heart is where the spirit is strong. An individual may find that their energy, their life force from within the heart has been disrupted, often due to life events. This will result in the energy flow becoming blocked. This often happens when there has been the loss of a loved one. It is almost as if the person has shut down and closed the heart. The wizard, the fire archetype tends to be quite sensitive and will equally close down when they feel disappointment and rejection in life. The opposite may also be true and a person who has the strong characteristics of the wizard may be too giving and considerate of others leaving themselves open to exploitation and abuse.

Useful crystals

Amber
This will help to strengthen the cardiac muscle as well as promoting unconditional love and releasing negative energy.

Black tourmaline
This stone will help to remove negativity from the heart caused by the individual themselves or by other people. Black tourmaline will also protect against psychic attack and therefore any negative energy from other people is less likely to be absorbed into the aura and the heart.

Emerald
This is a good stone to help combat hypertension (high blood pressure). This is a common condition for those who experience an imbalance in this area. Emeralds will also help support and develop relationships.

Blue Goldstone
This beautiful stone is said to be a great healer and can be used to heal and balance problems of the heart. The stone is best worn as a piece of jewellery, as a necklace if at all possible.

Black onyx

This is a wonderful stone for improving self-confidence and self-esteem. This stone is ideal for the wizard who may a little fragile and vulnerable at times.

White Topaz

This helps the wearer to maintain focus. All too often the wizard becomes absorbed in affairs of the heart. Losing focus of the big picture and taking the wrong path can lead the wizard to make some wrong decisions. By using/wearing this crystal the likelihood of this happening is reduced.

Lithium in quartz

This is a lovely calming crystal and can be used when the wizard becomes overwhelmed and develops anxiety. The gentle vibrations from the crystal will induce a state of calmness and control. Interestingly, the crystal is said to be self-cleansing, however I would suggest that you cleanse this crystal. By cleansing thoroughly you are ensuring, as far as possible that you are removing any build-up of negative energy.

Opal

These are lovely stones to help inspire an individual. At times the wizard will lack in inspiration and will feel quite deflated. Wearing an opal as a piece of jewellery or using an opal as part of a crystal healing session will help retrieve inspiration and a sense of balance is achieved once more. As opals contain a high proportion of water they have to be cleansed carefully. Do not use salt but instead cleanse with water or with a soft cloth containing oil. When wearing opal jewellery the wearer should remove the jewellery immediately if they feel any discomfort. As well as having the ability to inspire, opals have the ability to magnify the feelings of the user so, if a person is wearing opal jewellery and feels uncomfortable, the longer they continue to wear that piece of jewellery the worse they will feel.

Amethyst

This is a wonderful crystal to help inspire the creative. The wizard archetype greatly enjoys attracting the attention of others and partly being able to capture this attention is down to being creative with words. Amethyst will inspire the user to become verbally confident and creative.

Ruby

This crystal helps to aid the circulation as well as helping the digestive process. Health problems within the digestive tract occur when a person is unable to let go. A ruby will help to support the digestive and elimination process. Rubies also act as aphrodisiacs!

A crystal treatment to help balance energy flowing through the heart

In order to carry out this treatment you will need 10 crystals. Place the crystals in the following order:

- 1 crystal at the top of the head in line with the nose.
- 1 crystal between the eyebrows.
- 1 crystal on the throat.
- 1 crystal over the heart.
- 1 crystal parallel to the joint of each thumb.
- 1 crystal parallel to the joint of each small finger.
- 1 crystal on the outside of each arm, parallel to the armpit.

Please read through the previous section regarding treatment times and number of treatments. Always show consideration and respect the person you are treating. If they wish to stop the treatment or remove a particular crystal(s) please respect their wishes.

Earth

The peacemaker is the earth archetype and when healthy and well balanced she is loving, caring and practical. When imbalanced she is critical, harsh and uncaring. It is almost as if, at times, the peacemaker becomes overwhelmed with the tasks placed upon her.

Useful crystals

Black Kyanite
This crystal is from Brazil and is often used by Reiki healers. In Brazil it is called the witches broom. The crystal has a fan like shape and this enables the crystal to be used across a wide area of the body. This crystal can be used to induce calmness and tranquillity to a cluttered and busy mind and I use this crystal for grounding.

Blue Aragonite
Aragonite can be found in a number of colours, however blue aragonite can be used to help an individual become more connected to the spiritual aspect of themselves as well as the wider spiritual community. When those deeply connected to the earth become imbalanced they often become overly critical and this stone will help to re-balance the spirit from within.

Green Tourmaline
This is a lovely crystal to be used to connect a person to nature. If a person feels disconnected either through physical illness or mental stress this crystal will help them re-balance and connect with the world once more. Green tourmaline helps to promote love and empathy and the crystal itself has a very high vibrational frequency.

Smokey Quartz
This is a great crystal to help bring a person back to

earth and ground them. This crystal is ideal for the peacemaker to use when their mind wanders as well as being a lovely crystal to support healing. I often carry smokey quartz around with me in a pouch placed in my pocket as this is a light, but highly effective physically and mentally calming healing crystal.

Yellow Sapphire
This lovely gemstone can be used to treat physical problems related to the spleen and the stomach. These are common problems related to this archetype.

Cuprite
This lovely reddish brown stone is wonderful for emotional stability and grounding.

Black Obsidian
This is a crystal that can be used to cleanse psychic smog and to remove negativity. I believe that it is advisable for everyone to have a highly protective crystal that they use on a regular basis as this will help support a calm and tranquil mind.

Peridot
This crystal will help maintain and clear a person's thoughts as well as cleansing and protecting the aura.

Black Tourmaline
This crystal helps to purify the body and the mind by

removing mental and physical toxins. The user is able to connect with nature more easily, have increased compassion and love for those around them and have a high level of positive energy.

Citrine
This stone can help support the digestive system. It is lightweight to carry, removes negativity and is another ideal crystal for the peacemaker, who often encounters digestive problems from time to time.

A crystal healing treatment to help energy flow through the digestive system.
Number of crystals required: 8

- 1 crystal in between the eye brows (also known as the third eye).
- 1 crystal on the outside of the body parallel to each cheekbone.
- 1 crystal over the heart.
- 1 crystal over the stomach area.
- 1 crystal in between the legs.
- 1 crystal at the heel of the foot parallel to the second toe.

Please be aware of the treatment times and instructions noted earlier on in this book.

Metal

The alchemist is the archetype associated with the metal element. Structure, order and the value of other people, the alchemist is the only archetype who truly is unconcerned with the material worth of another human being. When imbalanced there are a number of physical symptoms such as back problems and headaches as well as irritable bowel syndrome, which need to be addressed in order to restore good health.

Useful crystals

Agate

This is a great stone for calming the mind and reducing the likelihood of an irritable bowel flare up. The mind affects the body in many ways and by allowing the mind to stay calm there is less chance that the body will have a reaction that could cause a flare up of irritable bowel syndrome.

Citrine

Citrine is a great crystal to help the whole of the digestive system including flare up's of irritable bowel syndrome as well as helping to support your mind by keeping you calm and relaxed.

Bloodstone

This stone will help to strengthen determination as well as support those with low self-esteem.

Black Onyx

This is a crystal which can support any metal types who are distracted and have problems achieving their goals. One of the difficulties that the alchemist has is that he may be too giving and take on board the difficulties of others too readily. Black onyx will offer protection from taking on too much.

Chalcedony

This is considered to be a special stone by Native American Indians. This stone, which is part of the quartz family, can be used to help promote compassion and empathy. This is idea for those alchemists who feel as if they have lost their way and their trust in other people.

Amethyst

This is a wonderful crystal to help reduce headaches. Try carrying around some amethyst in a pouch in your pocket. This will work with the vibrations of your body, aligning them to a healthy high frequency. When you carry crystals around with you each time you put your hand on them in your pocket or touch them, you will comforted and reminded of their healing potential.

Apatite

This crystal is great for pain relief and may be used to help a frozen shoulder. Please remember, that this book is not intended as substitute for professional medical support and if a person is in pain they should seek advice from a suitably qualified medical professional.

Amber
This is a lovely stone to help the alchemist focus and have a clear mind.

Malachite
This is great for back pain. Many alchemist types do develop back pain at some point. Malachite is also useful for reducing the pain associated with inflammatory arthritis.

Moonstone
This can be used to bring love and empathy. At times, when the alchemist is imbalanced, he may find that it is difficult to develop a connection with loved ones and friends. Moonstone will help to turn that around and bring a greater sense of connection once more.

A crystal healing treatment to help energy flow through the stomach
Number of crystals needed: 10

- 1 crystal at the top of the head.
- 1 crystal parallel to the middle of each ear.
- 1 crystal each side of the head , half way between the ears and the crystal at the top of the head.

- 1 crystal on the throat.
- 1 crystal over the stomach area.
- 1 crystal between the top of the legs.
- 1 crystal in the middle of each heel.

Treatment time: As with all of the other treatments, begin with between 15 and 30 minutes for the first session and gradually increase by 5 minutes each session as the number of treatments progresses to a maximum of 50 minutes.

Water

The water archetype is the philosopher. Kidney and bladder problems are associated with this archetype as well as the inability to let go of grief and sadness. The crystals chosen below are specifically selected to help support water types in becoming healthier and well balanced physically and mentally.

Useful crystals

Red Calcite
This will help increase mental and physical energy, as well as enabling the user to move on and not focus on past events.

Orange Calcite
This stone helps to remove fear. The emotion of fear,

due to what has happened and what may happen, can paralyse the philosopher and prevent healthy emotional, physical and spiritual growth.

Sunstones

These stones, as the name suggests, enable to user to feel happier and more fulfilled.

Rhodonite

This will help lift the mood of those who experience impatience. The philosopher is prone to impatience at times and this crystal is ideal in helping support mental balance.

Rose Quartz

This is a lovely stone to enable to user to open up the heart and allow fear and grief to be addressed either through professional therapy and/or reflection and support from family and friends.

Watermelon Tourmaline

This is one of my favourite crystals! The colours are the same of that of a water melons three colours, namely green, pink and white in varying proportions. The crystal attracts love and commitment.

Garnet

This will allow the heart to become more open and attract love reducing loneliness.

Tigers Eye

This helps to maintain balance between the heaven and the earth, between night and day. The philosopher needs to achieve this balance and see the world for what it and not be stuck in the past.

Zebra Jasper

This lovely stone has markings of black and white, like a zebra. The crystal will help to turn thoughts into action by energising and motivating.

Aqua Marine

This crystal will help promote courage and allow the user/wearer to move on with their lives.

A crystal healing treatment to help energy flow through the kidneys and bladder

Number of crystals needed: 9

- 1 crystal at the middle of the sole of each foot.
- 1 crystal at the inside of each knee.
- 1 crystal at the top of the legs.
- 1 crystal over the stomach area.
- 1 crystal over the heart.
- 1 crystal over the throat.
- 1 crystal at the top of the head.

Treatment times: Between 15 and 30 minutes for the first session. Please see the advice earlier on in this book.

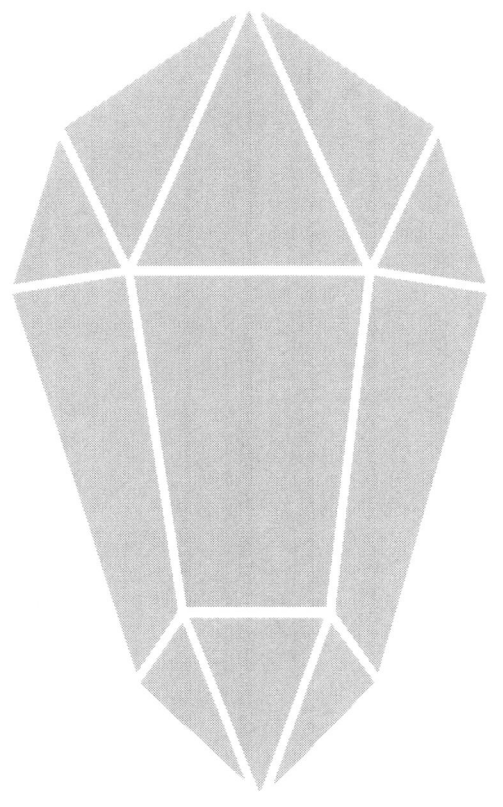

ALSO BY MARION MCGEOUGH

If you have enjoyed reading this book you may also be interested in the following:

Crystal Healing and the Human Energy Field: A Beginners Guide.

A Beginner's Guide to the Chakras.

Shoden: The definitive guide to first degree Reiki: Mindfulness, Meditation, Reiki treatments and more.

A Beginner's Guide to Mindfulness.

A Beginner's Guide to Developing Your Intuition.

Hypnosis CD: Overcome Your Fear of Flying.

All products are available from Amazon. If you wish to contact Marion here are her details.

marionreiki@yahoo.co.uk

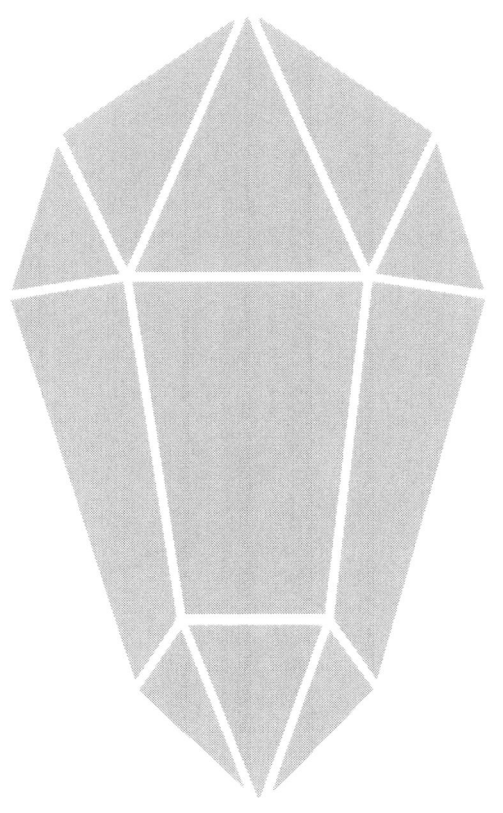

Printed in Great Britain
by Amazon